THIS BO
BELONGS TO

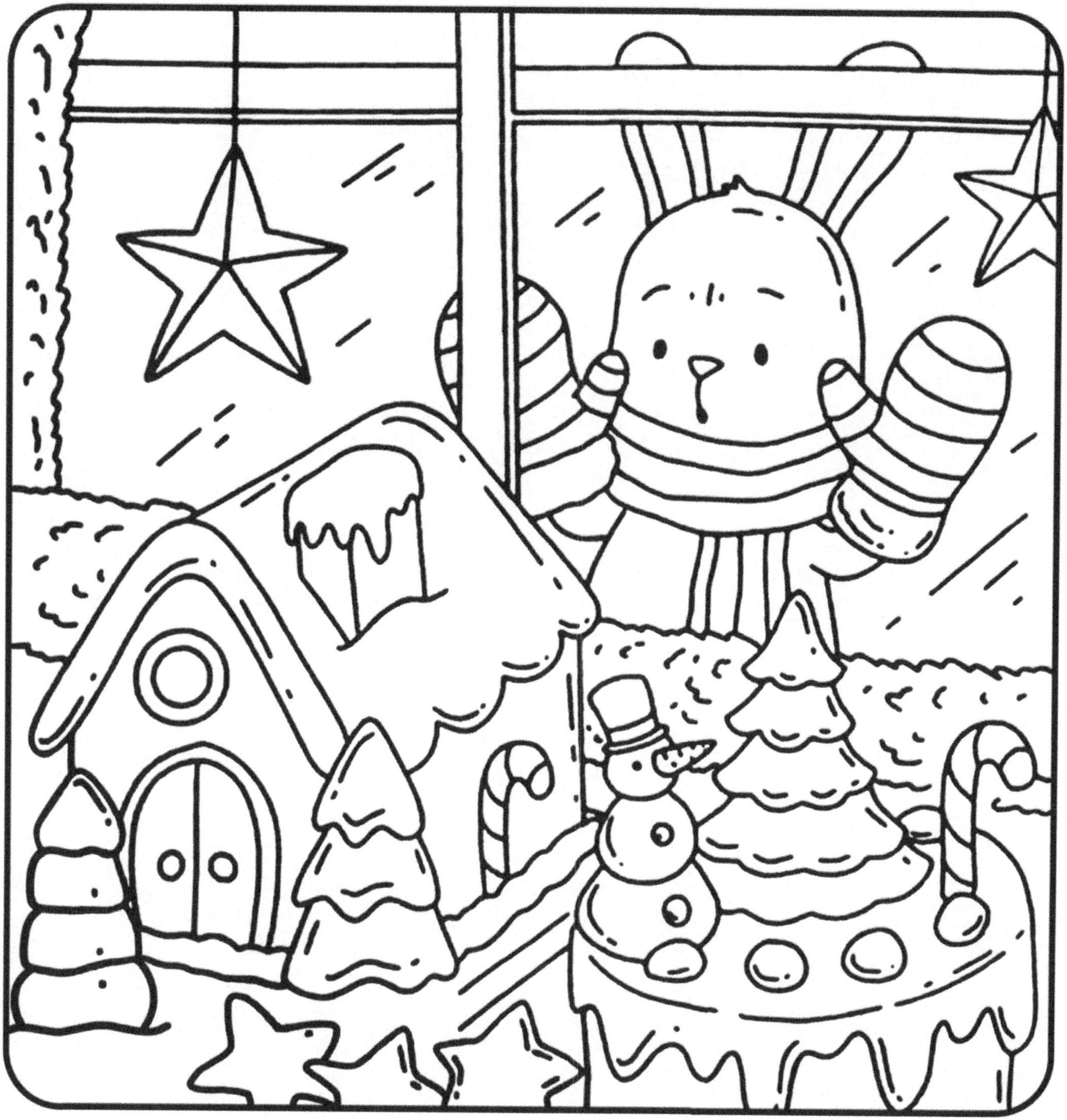

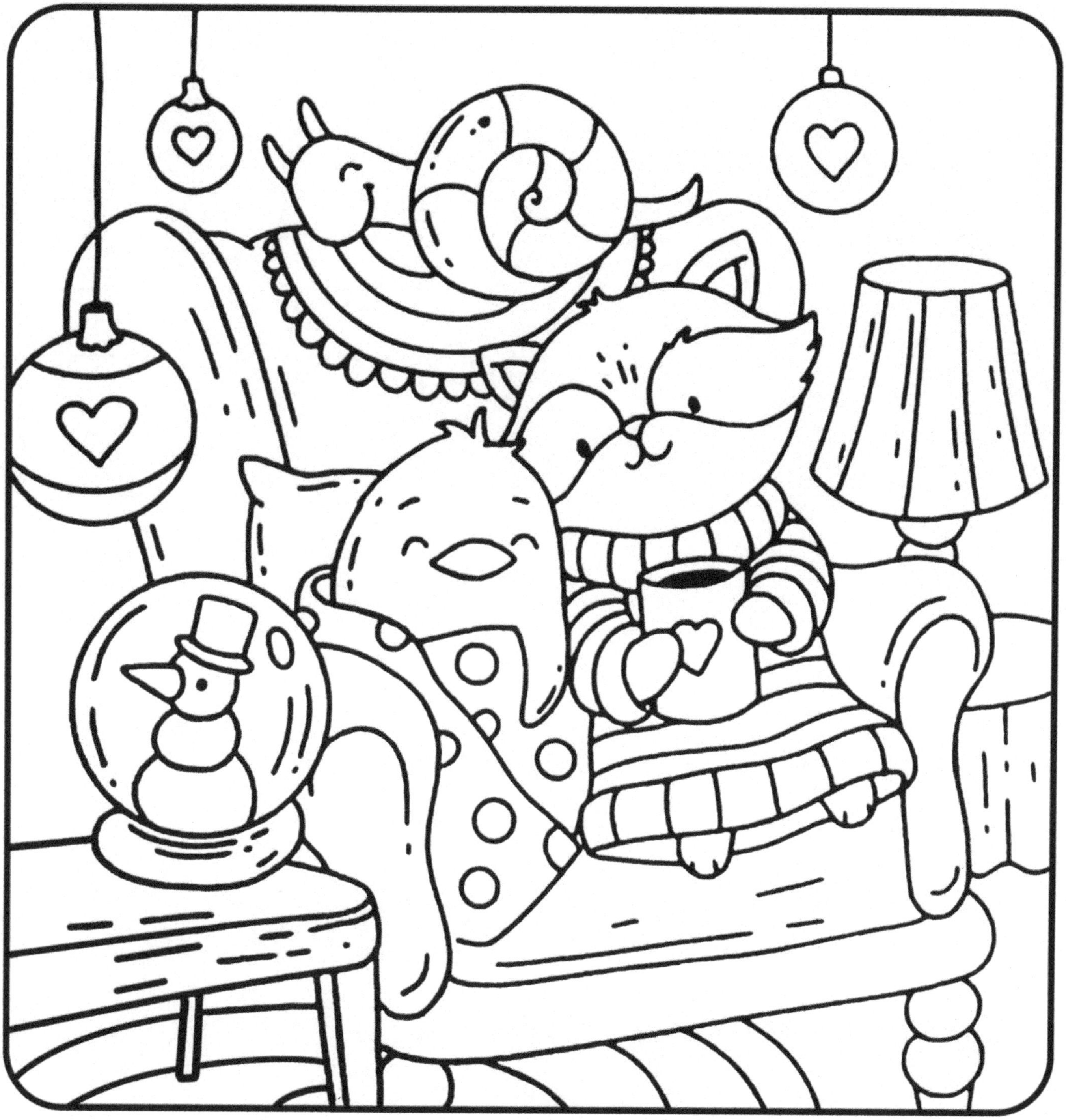

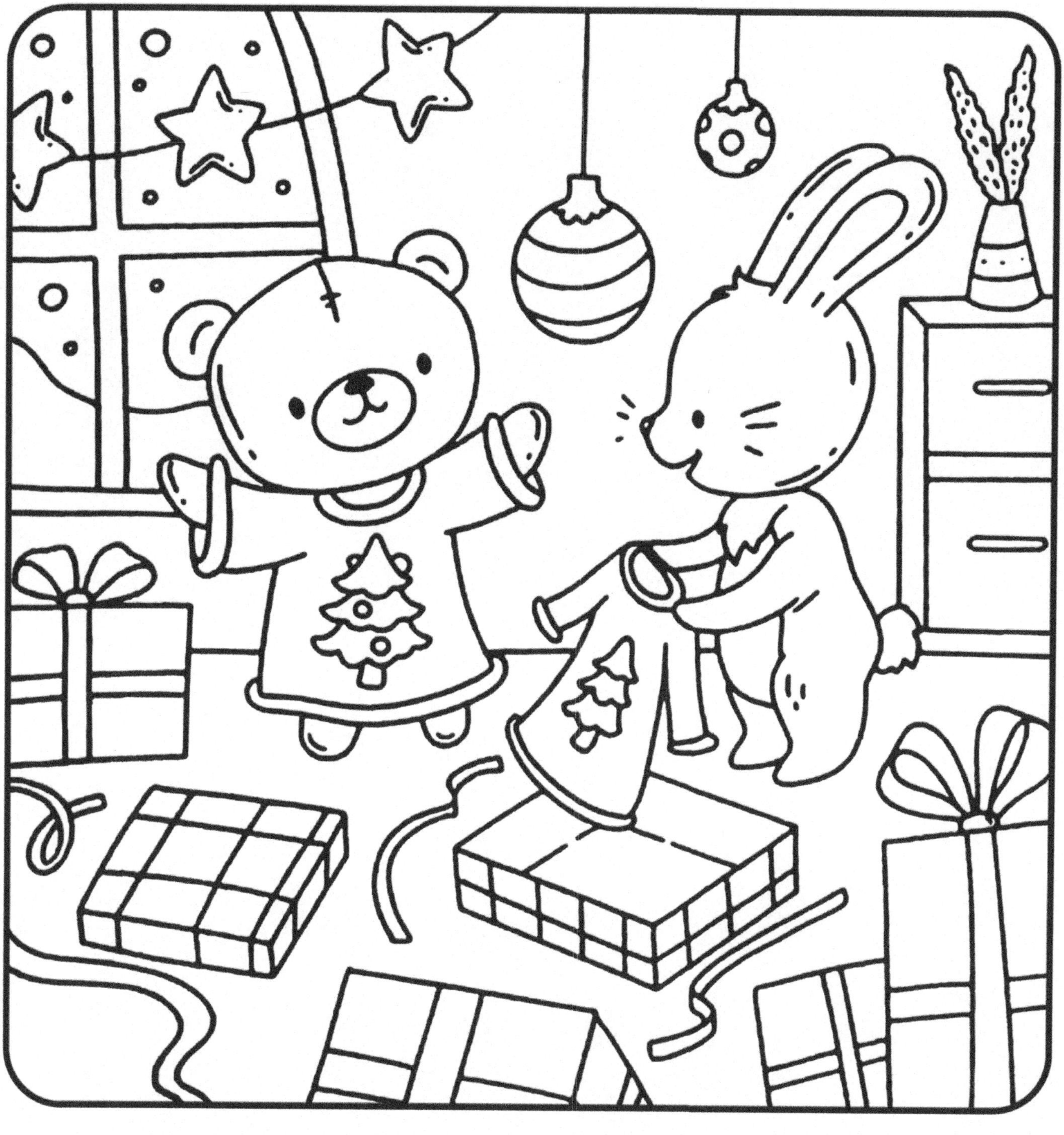

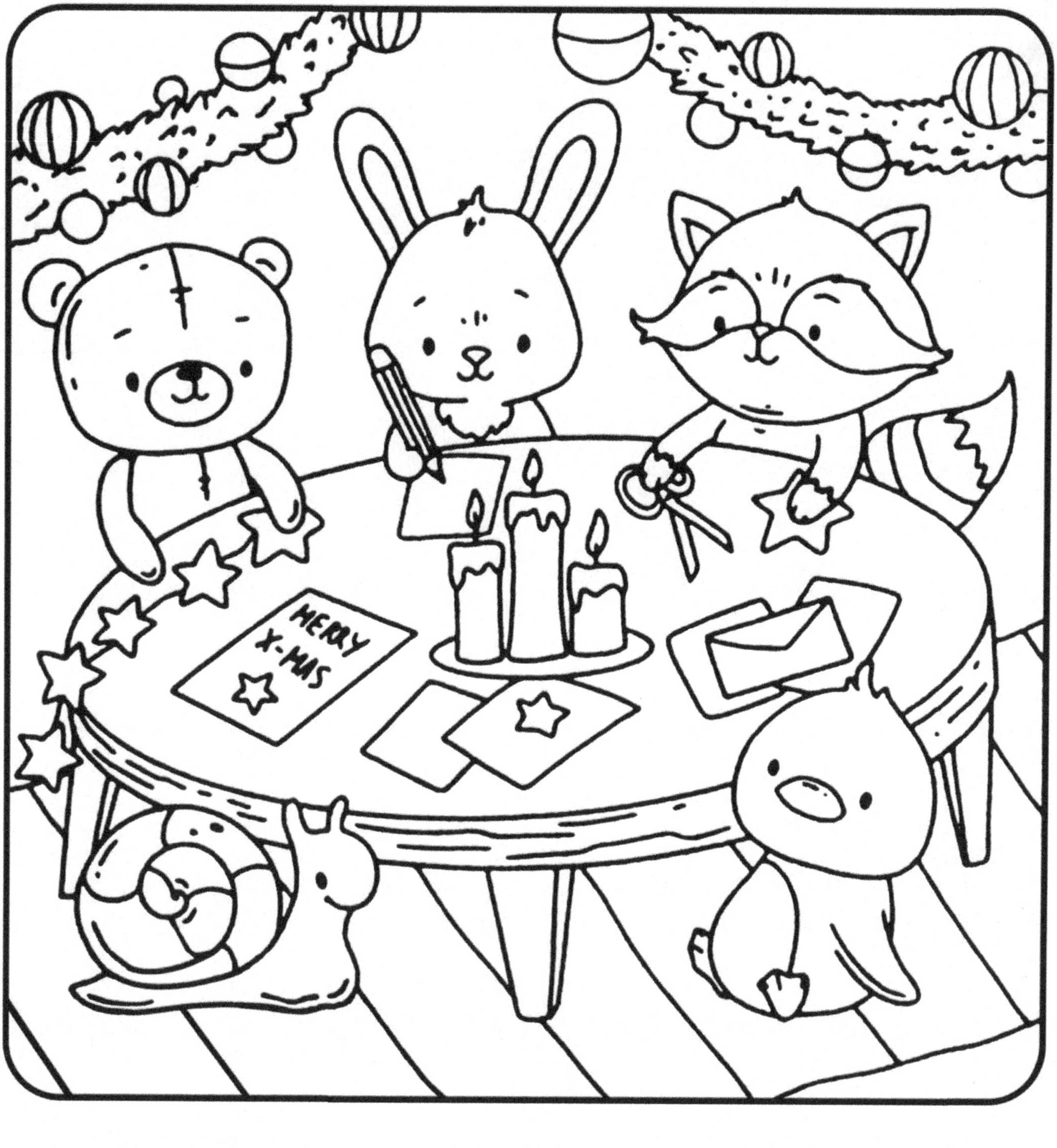
MERRY
X-MAS

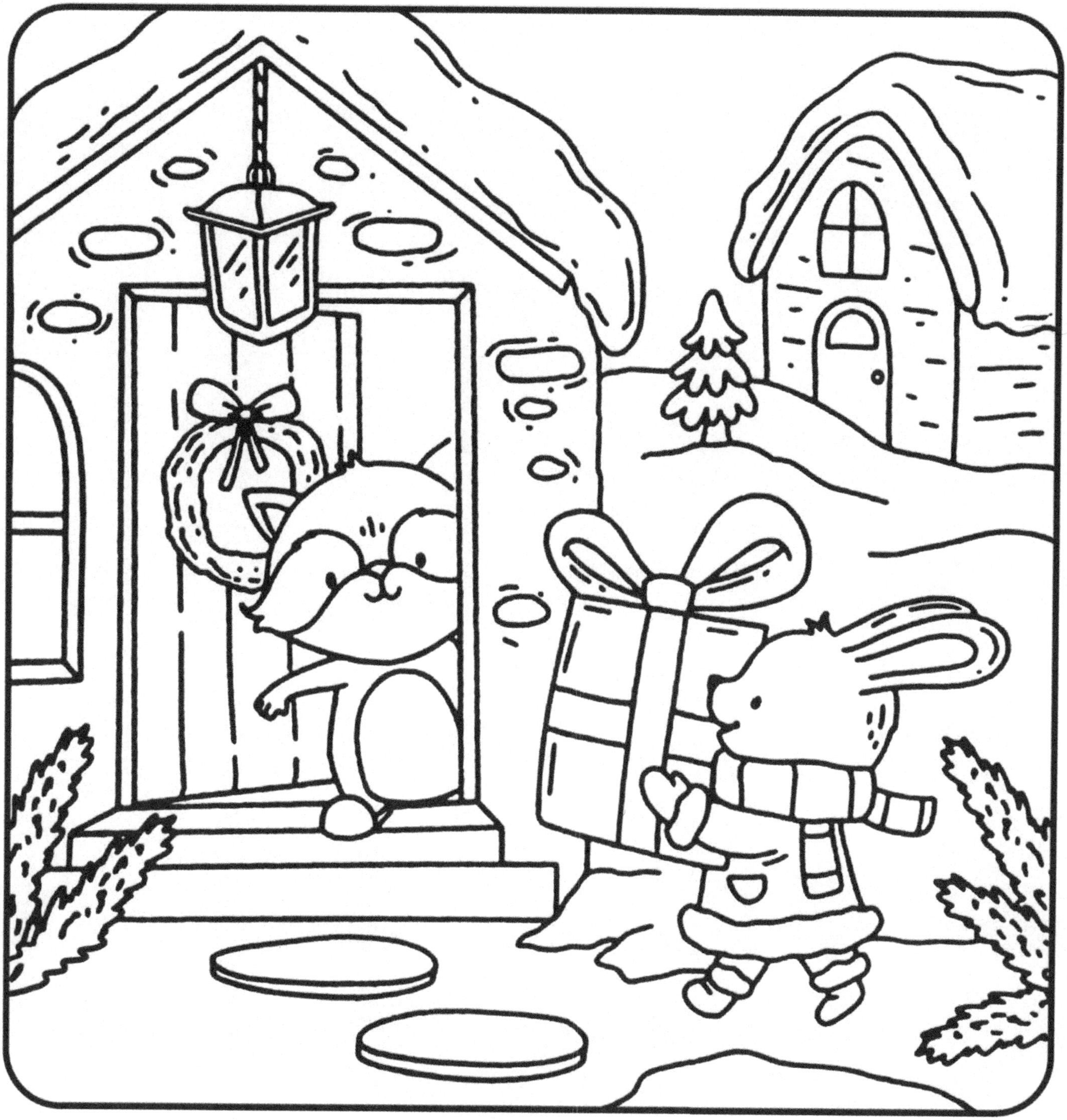

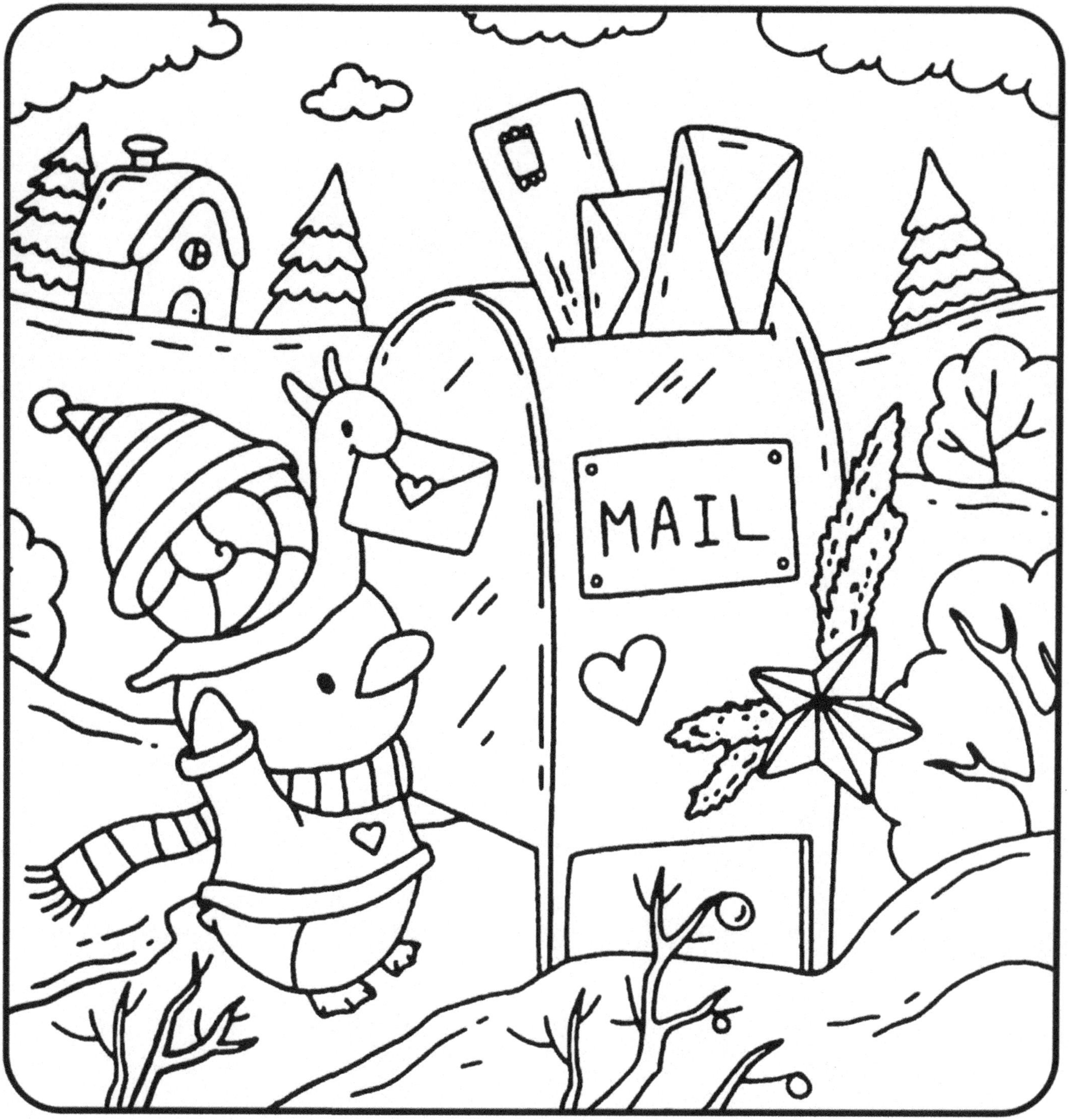
MAIL

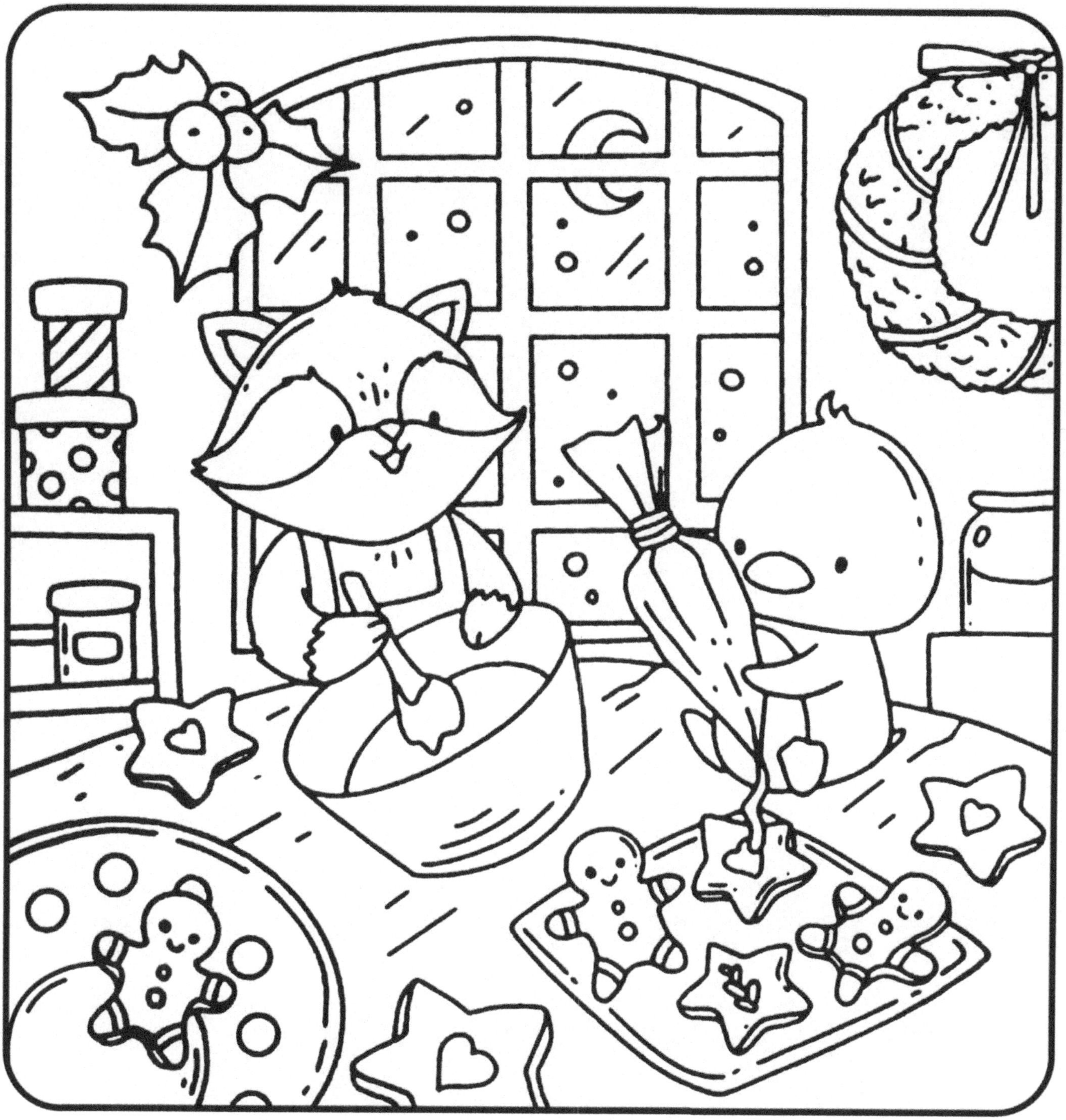

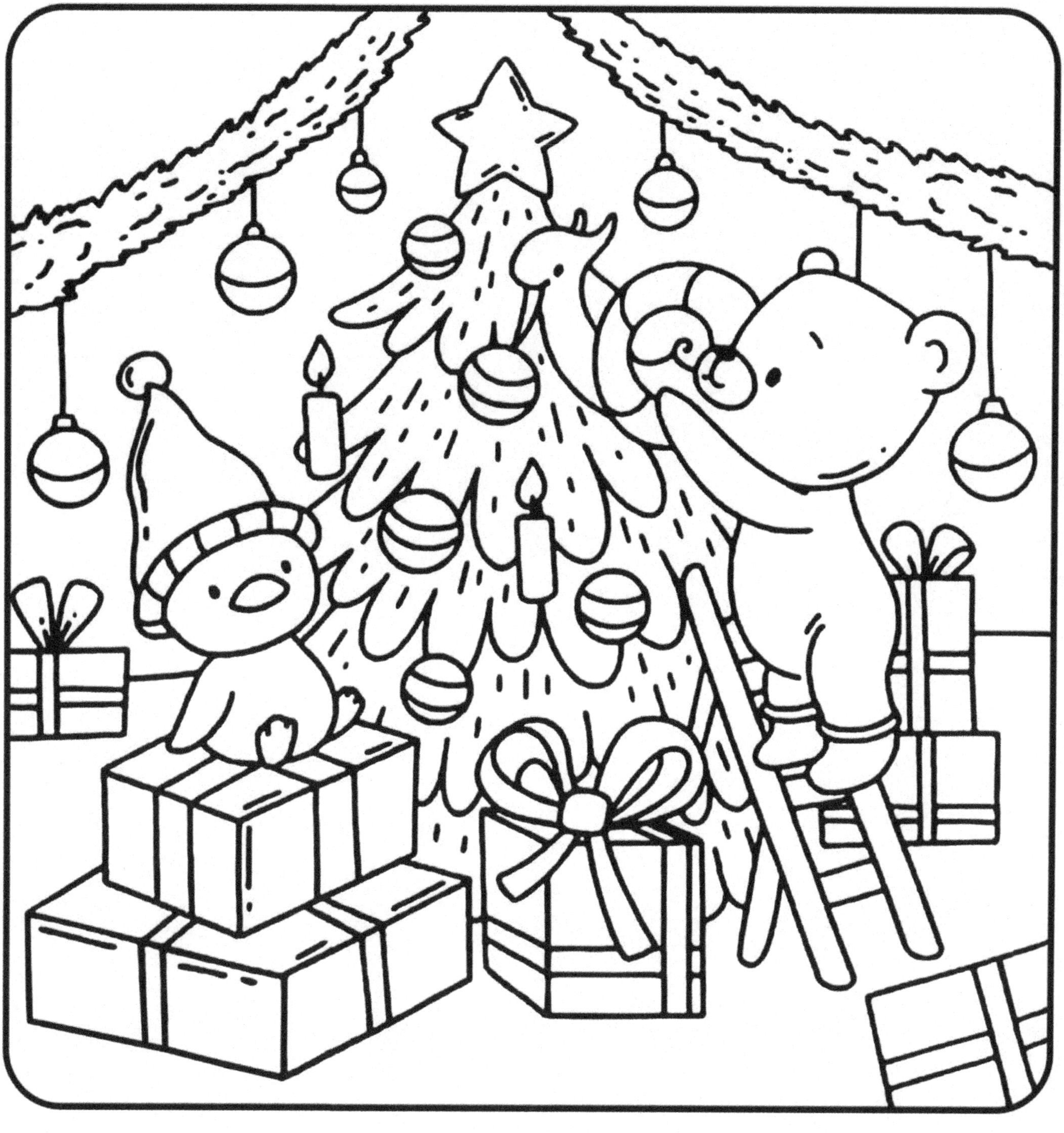

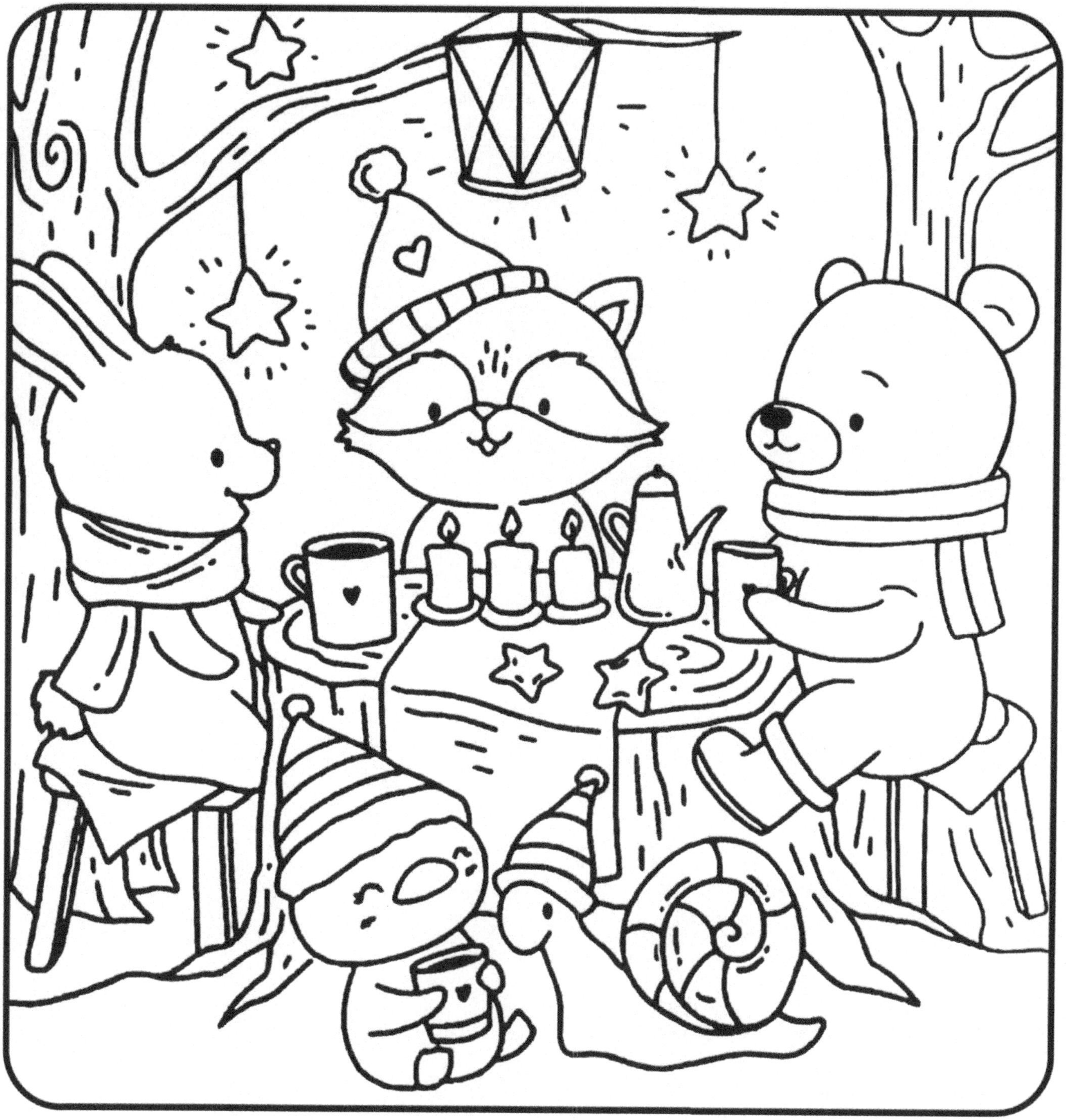

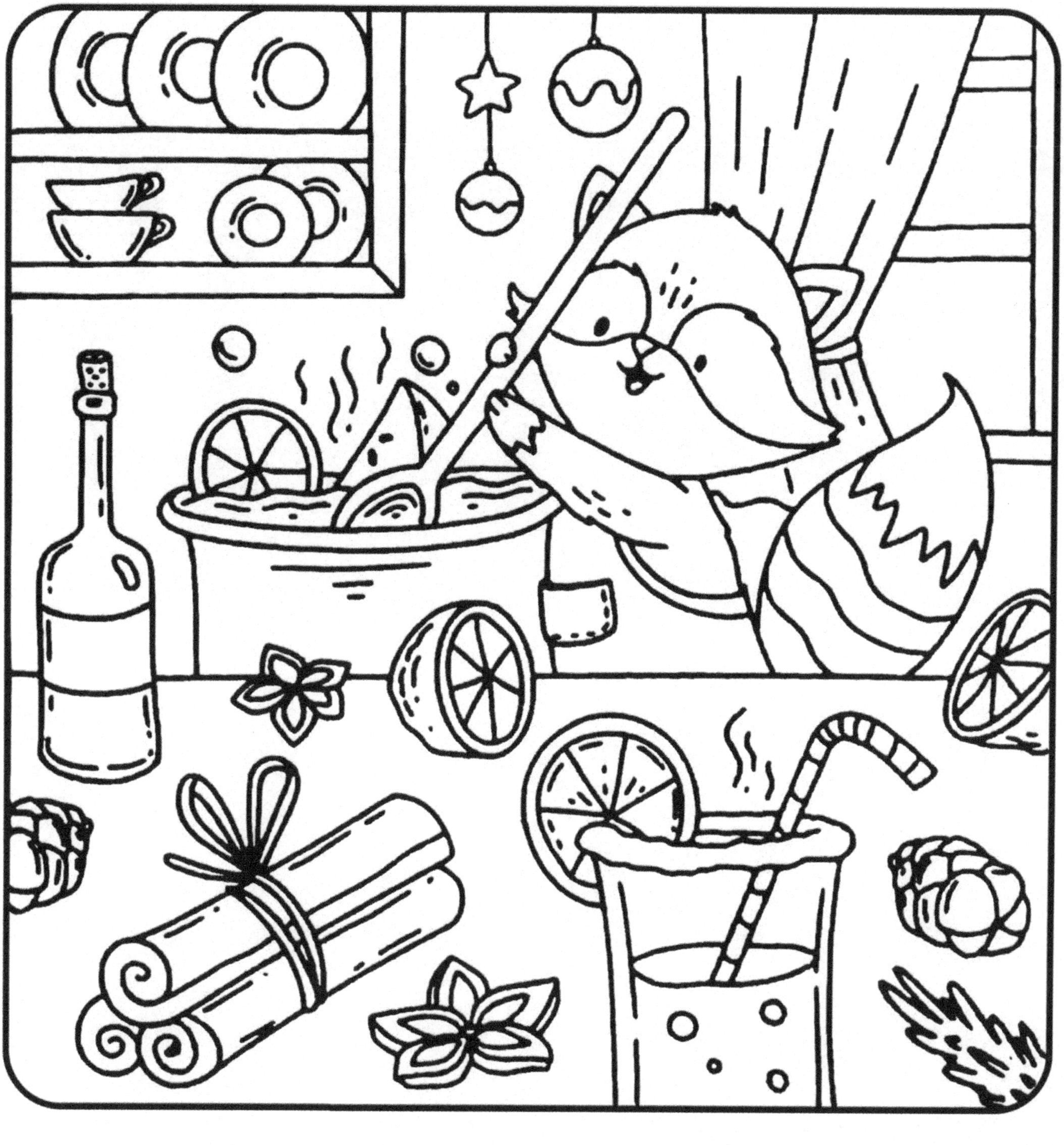

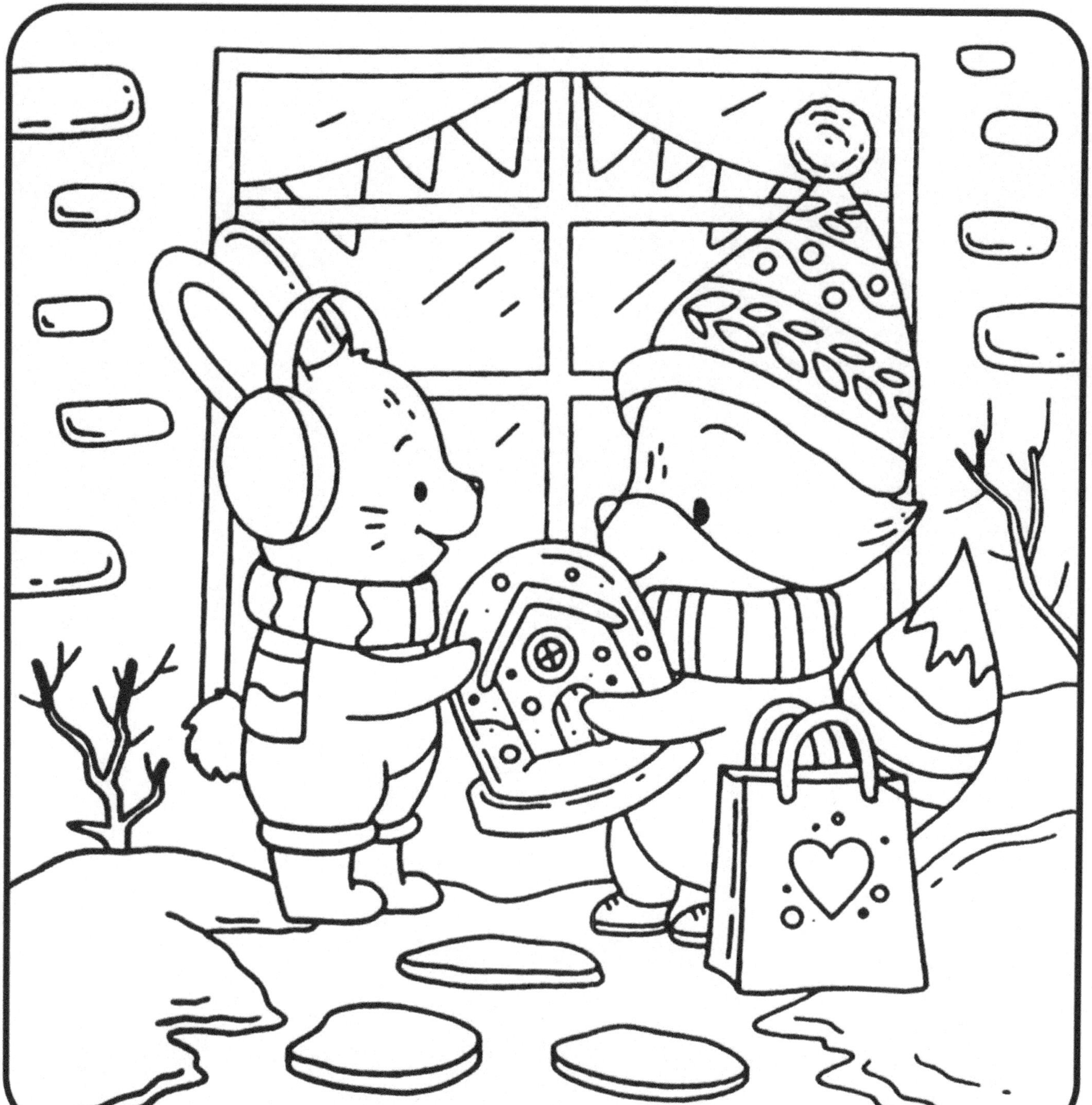

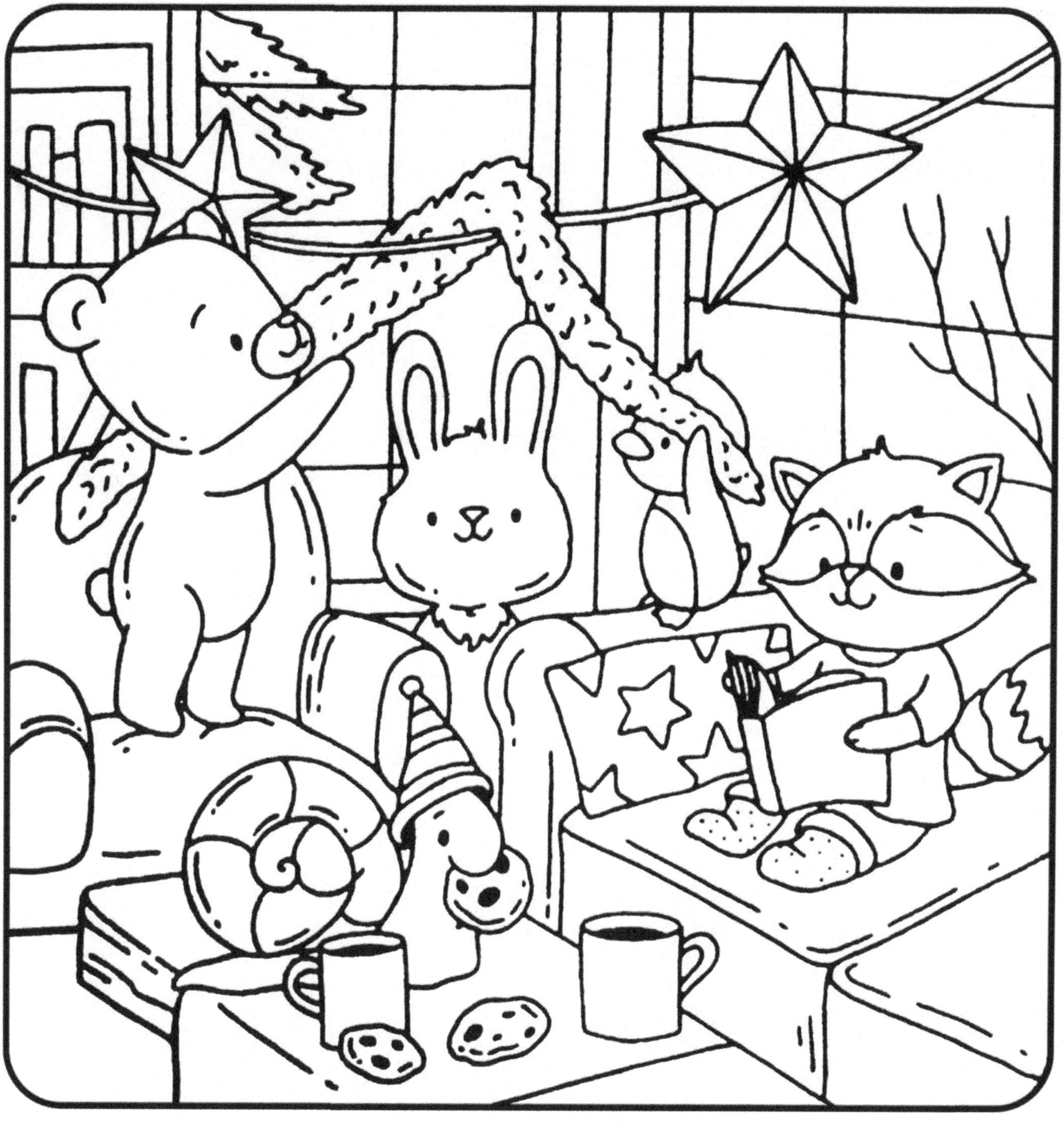

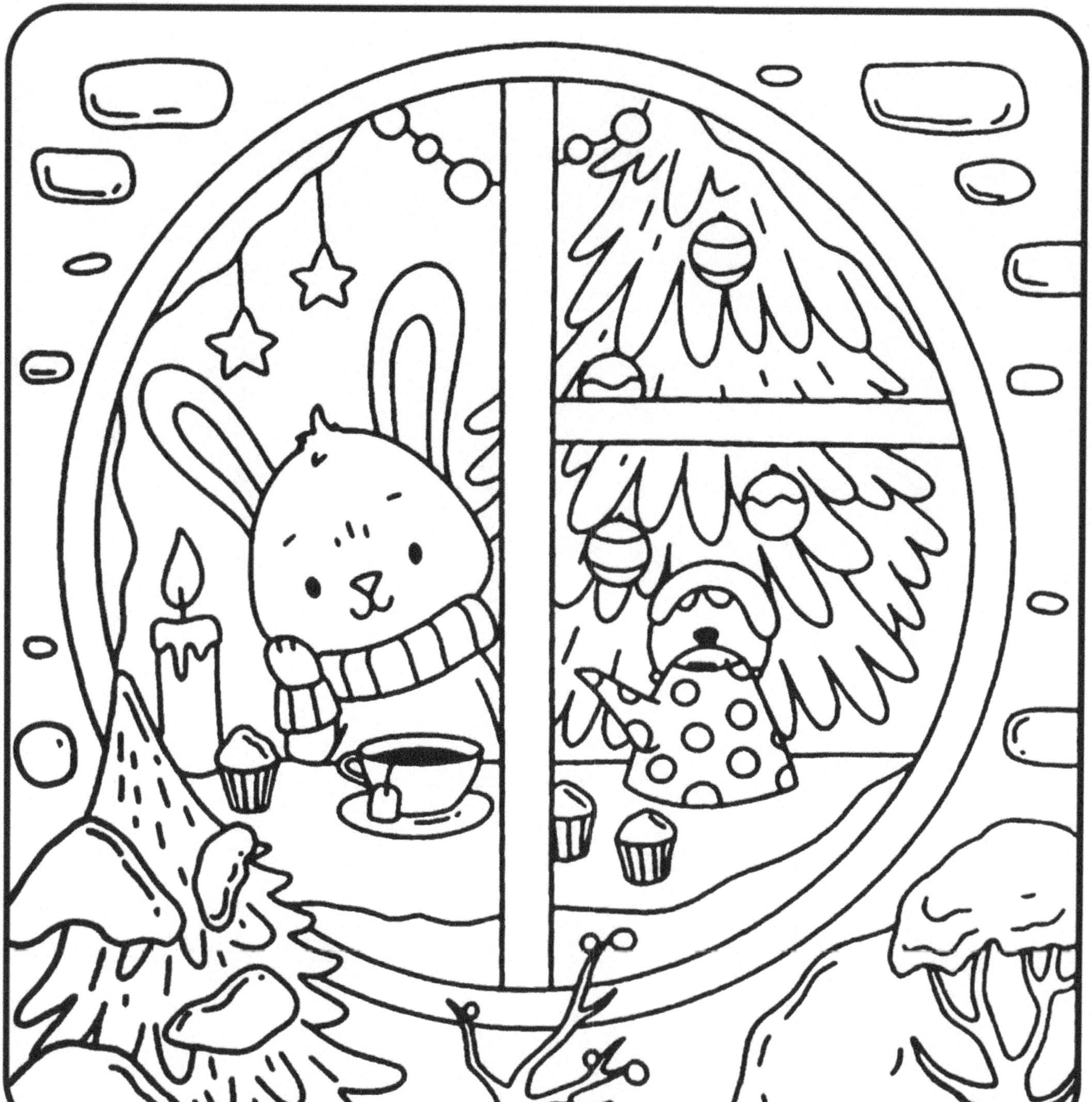

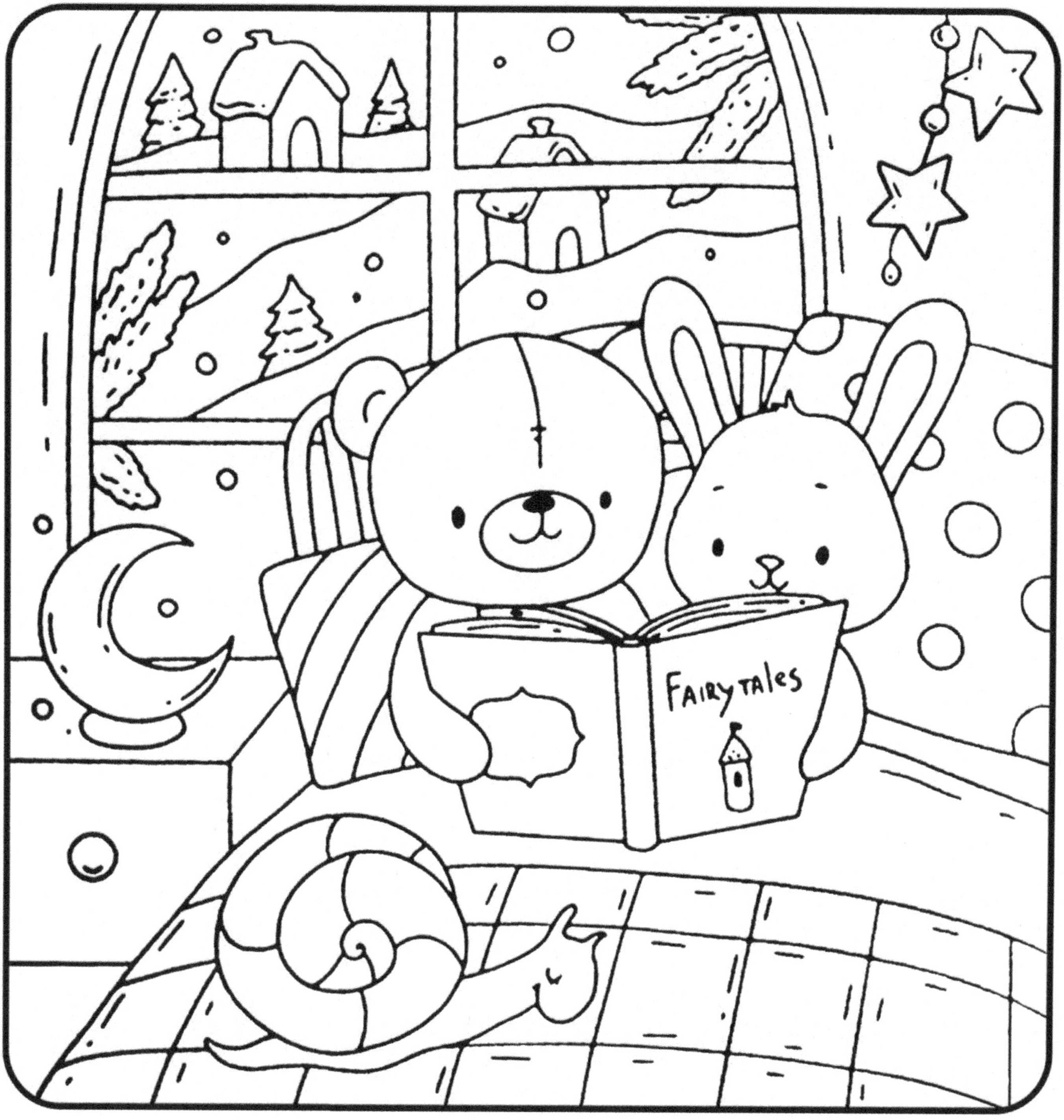
FAIRY TALES

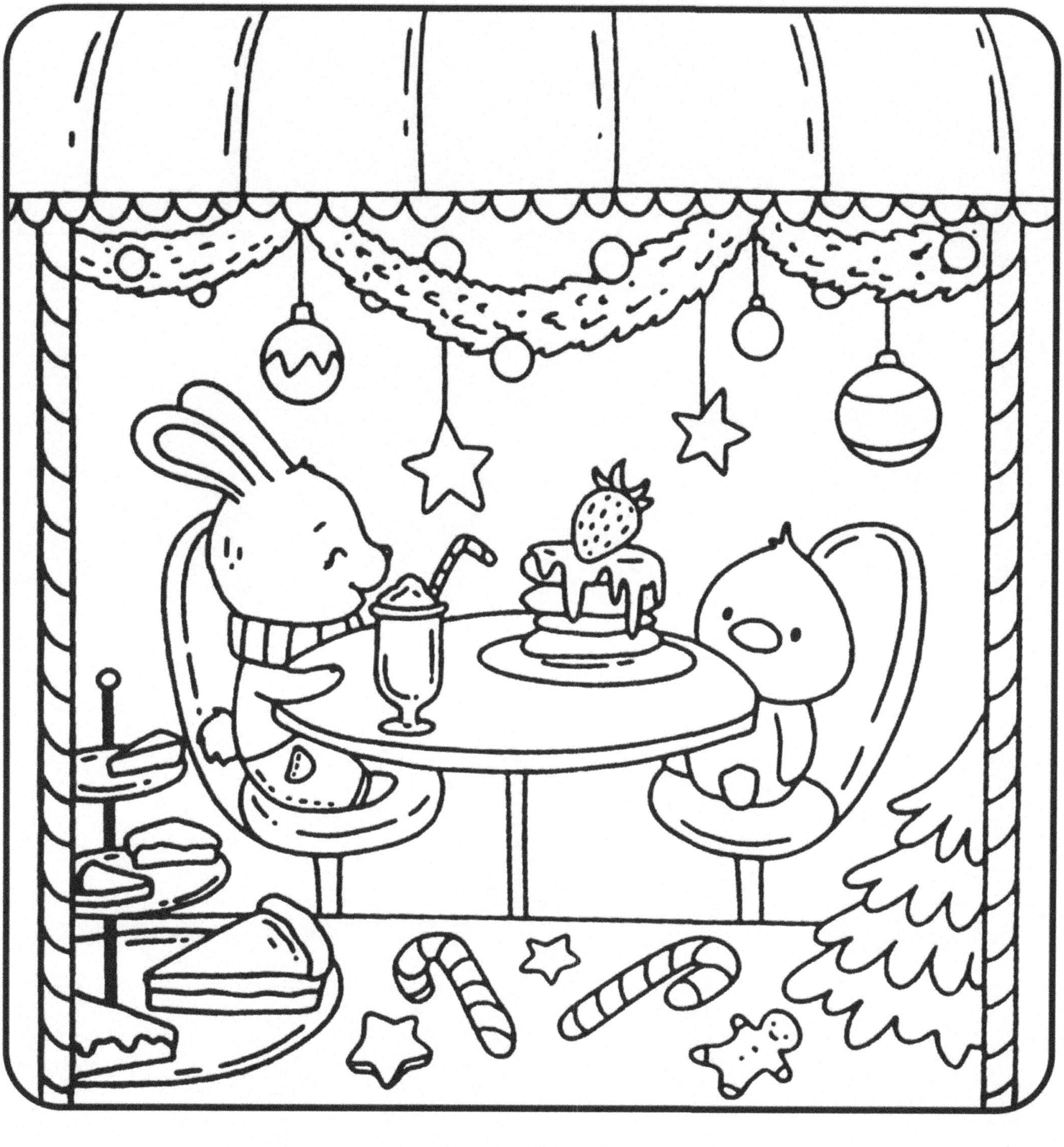

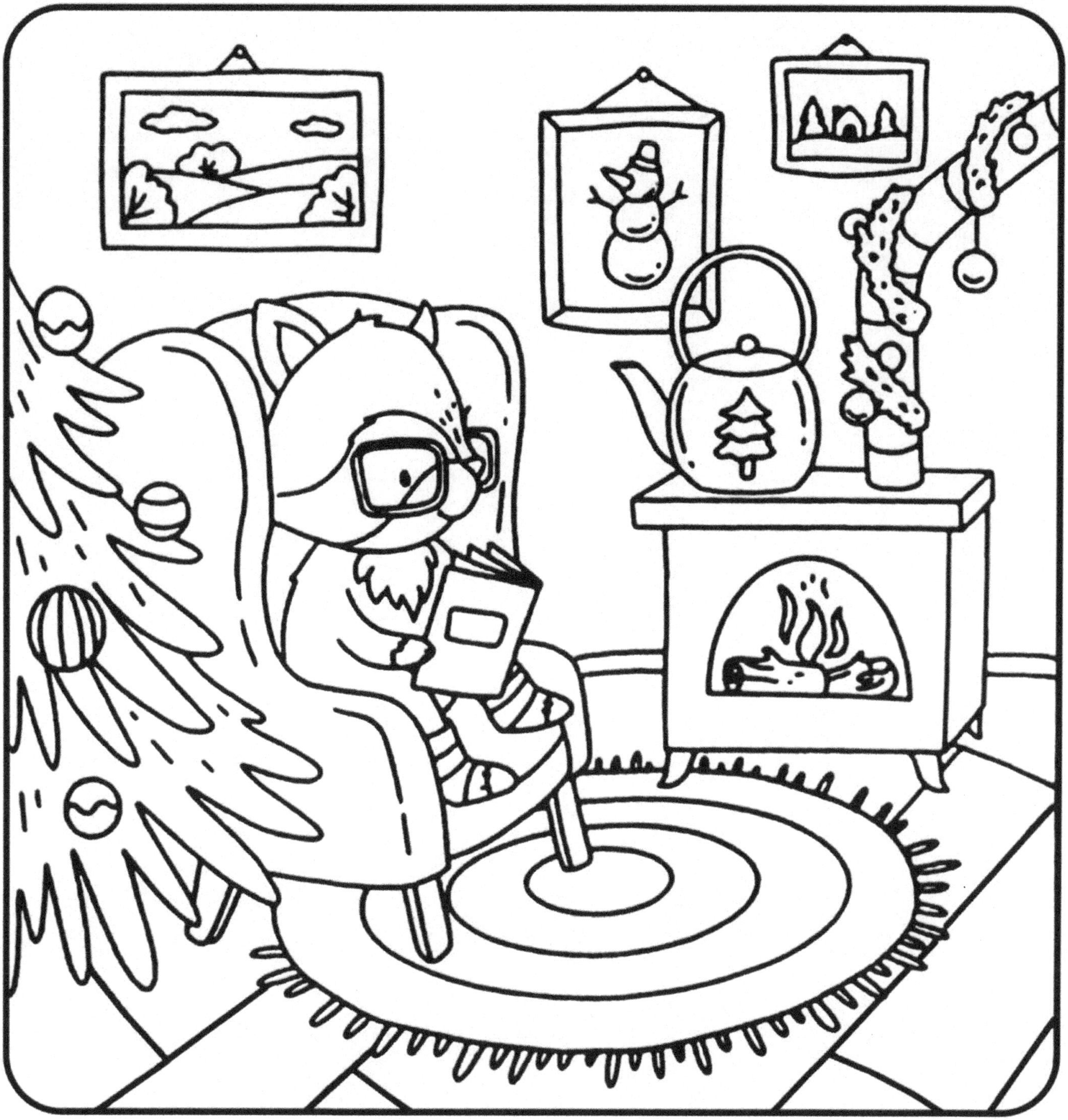

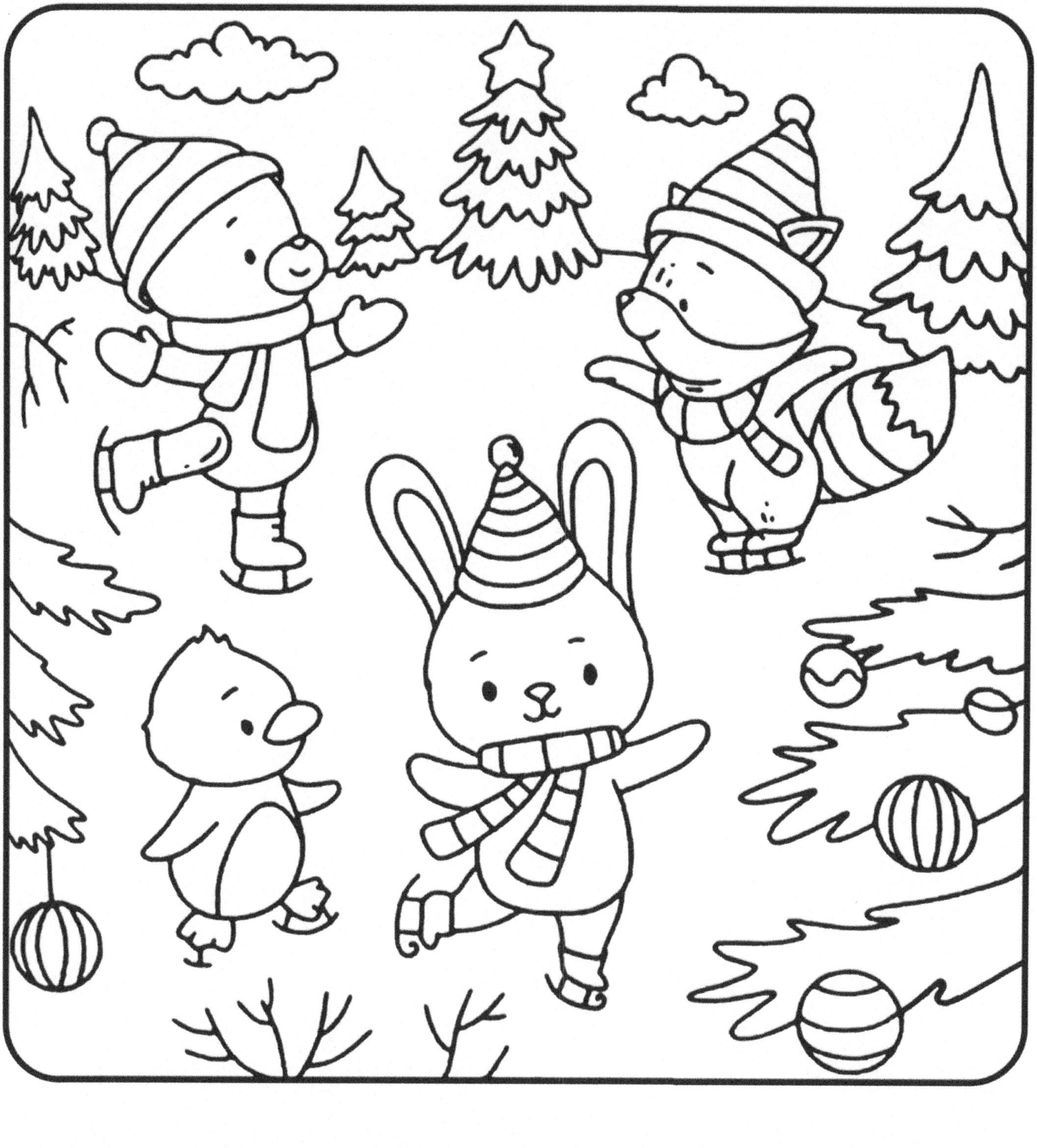

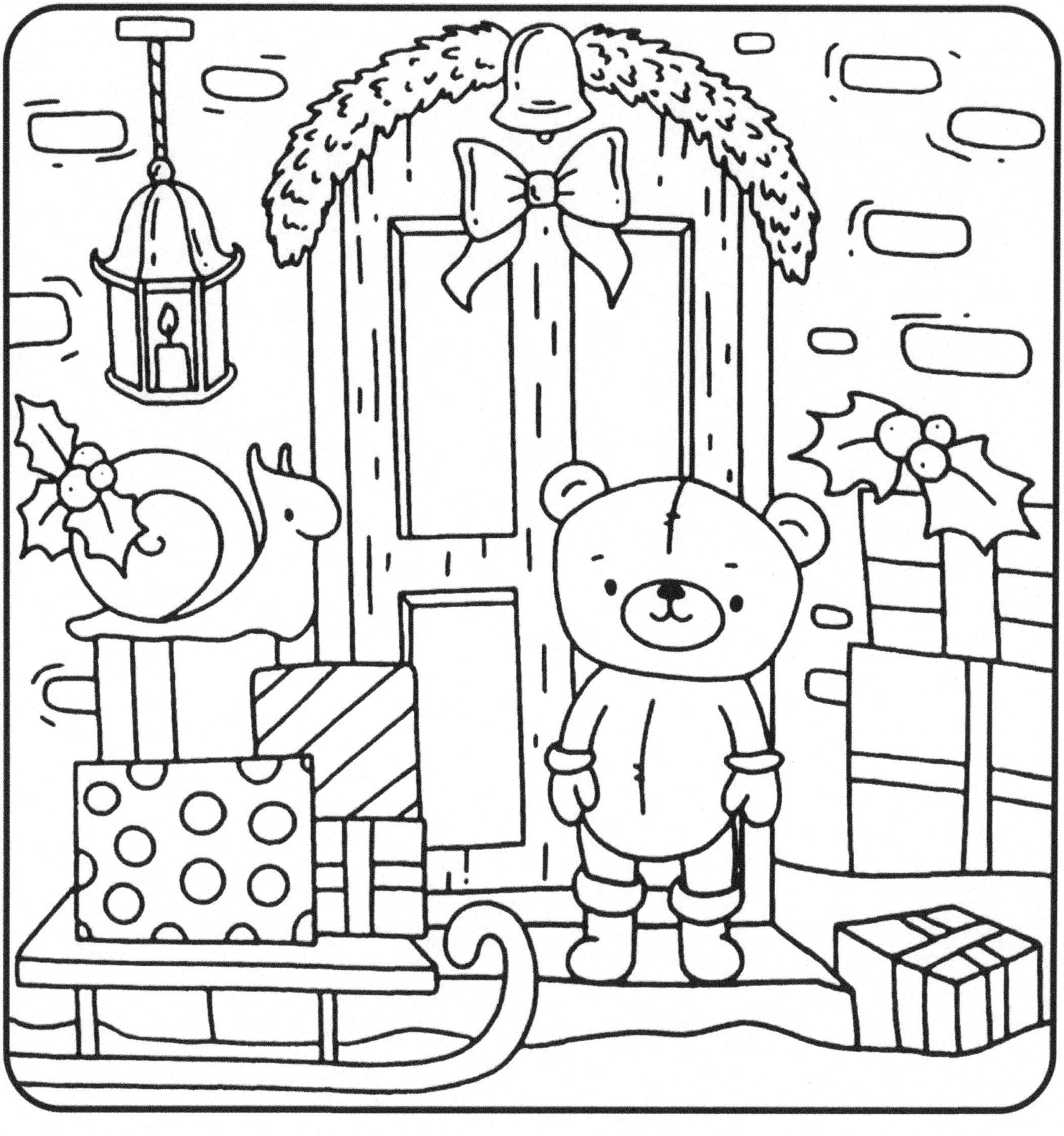

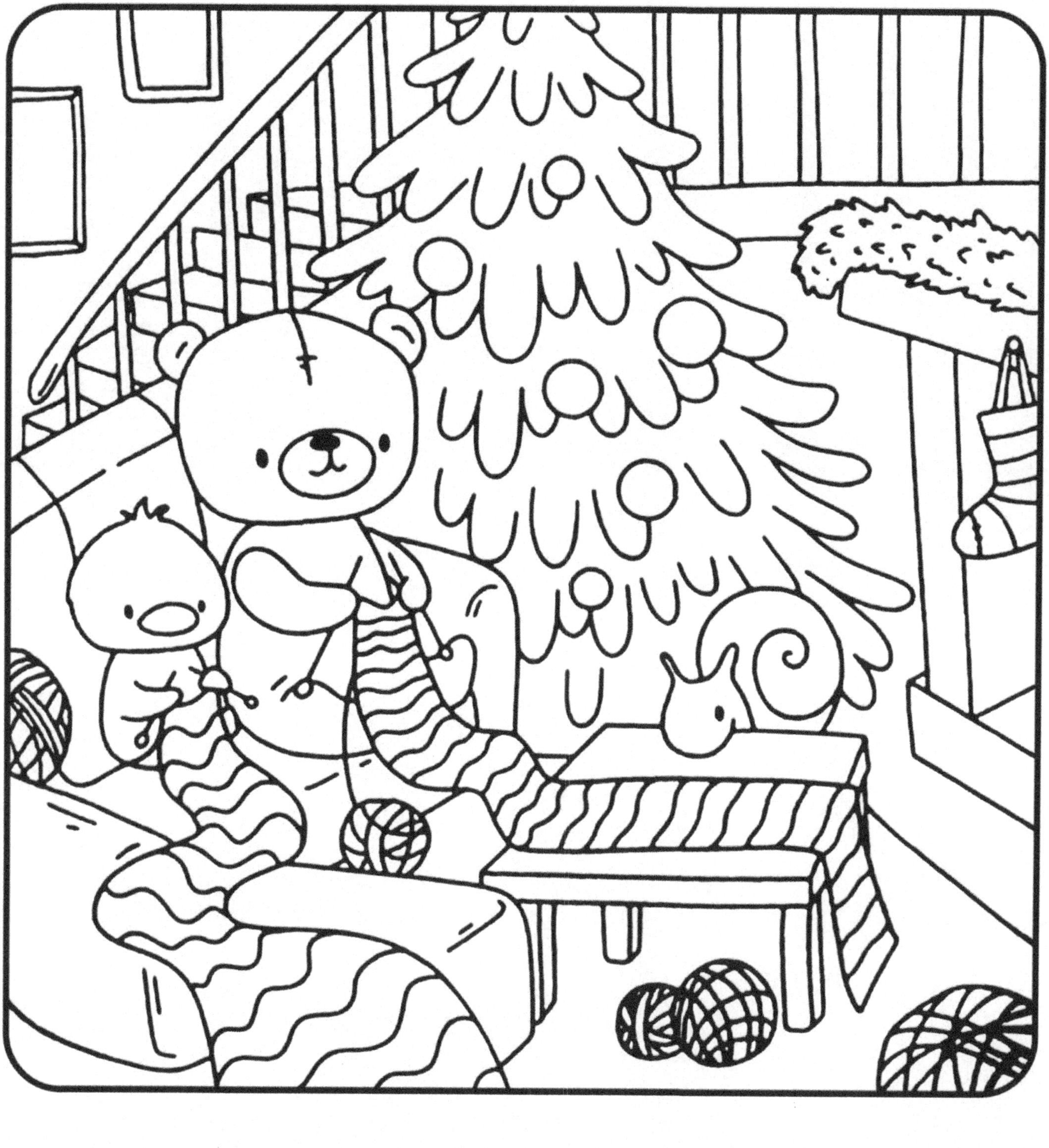

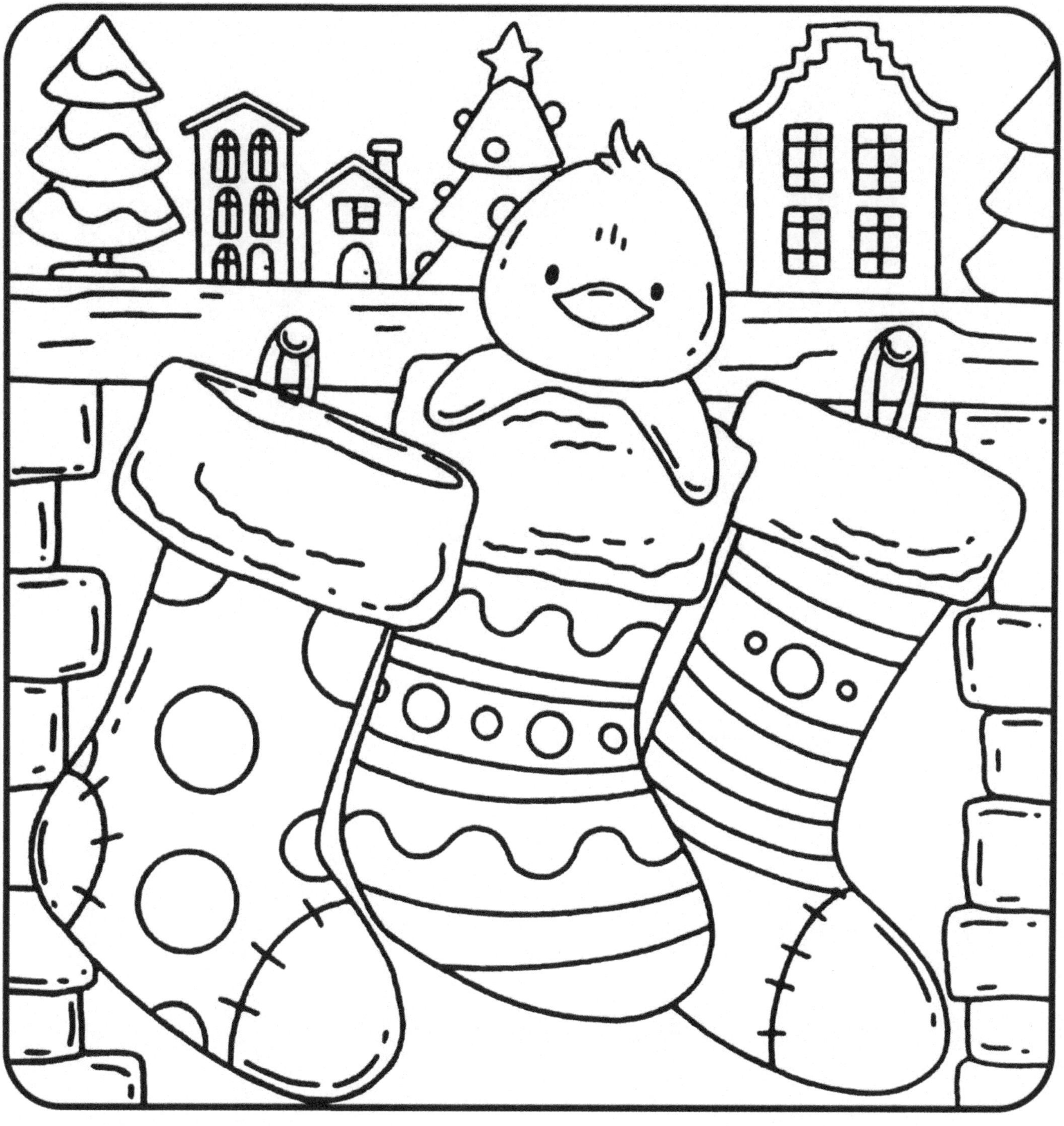

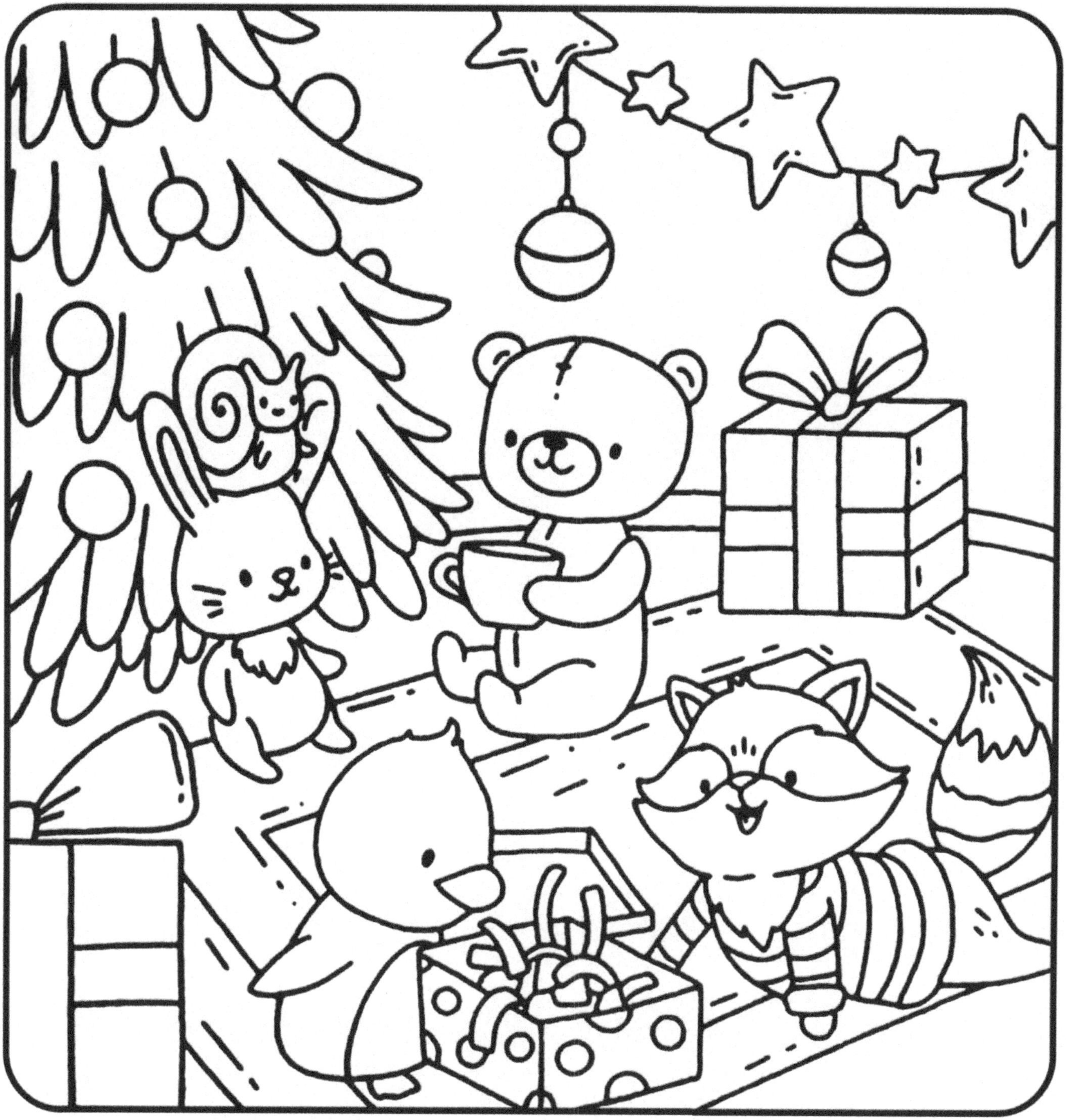

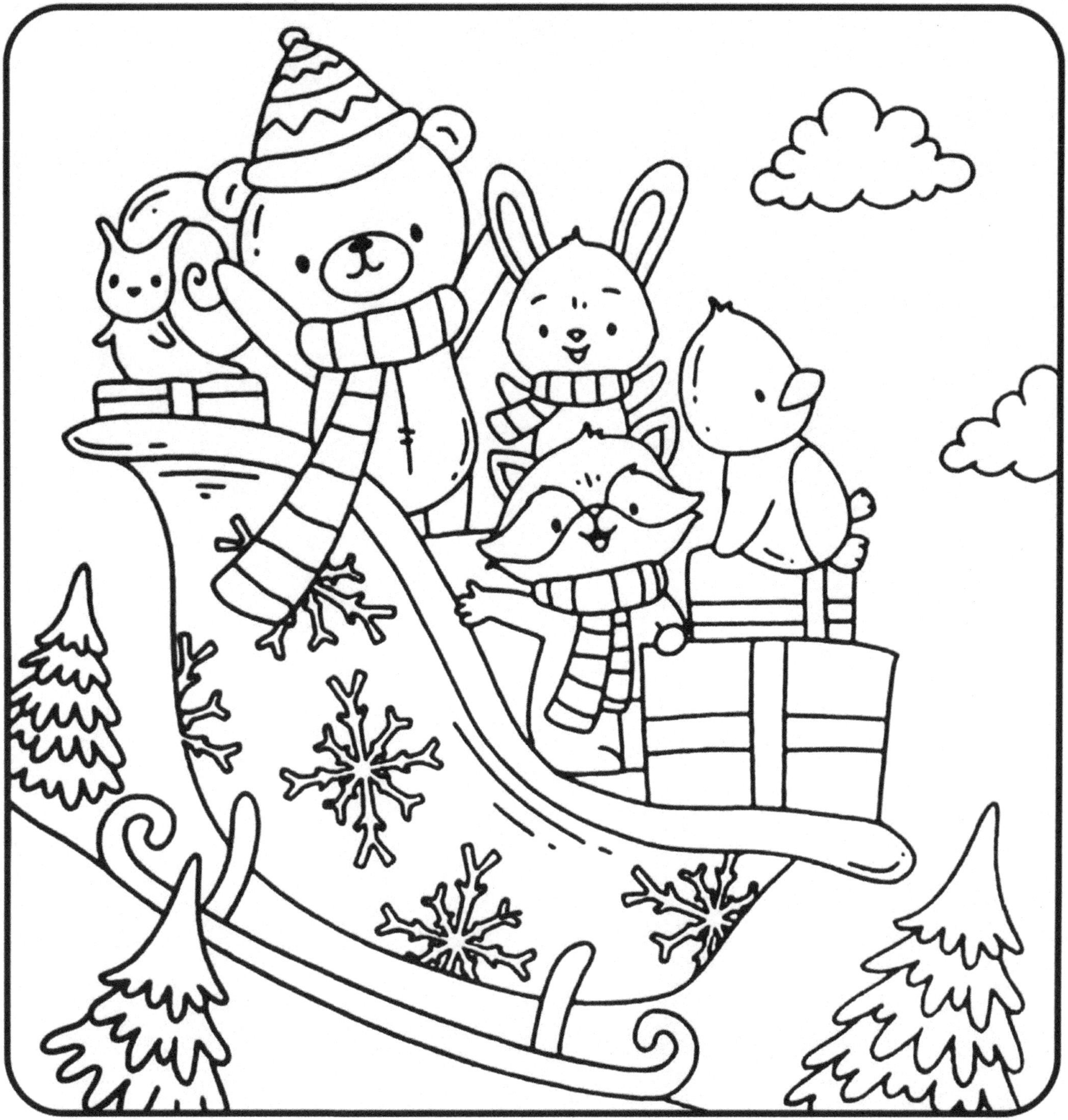

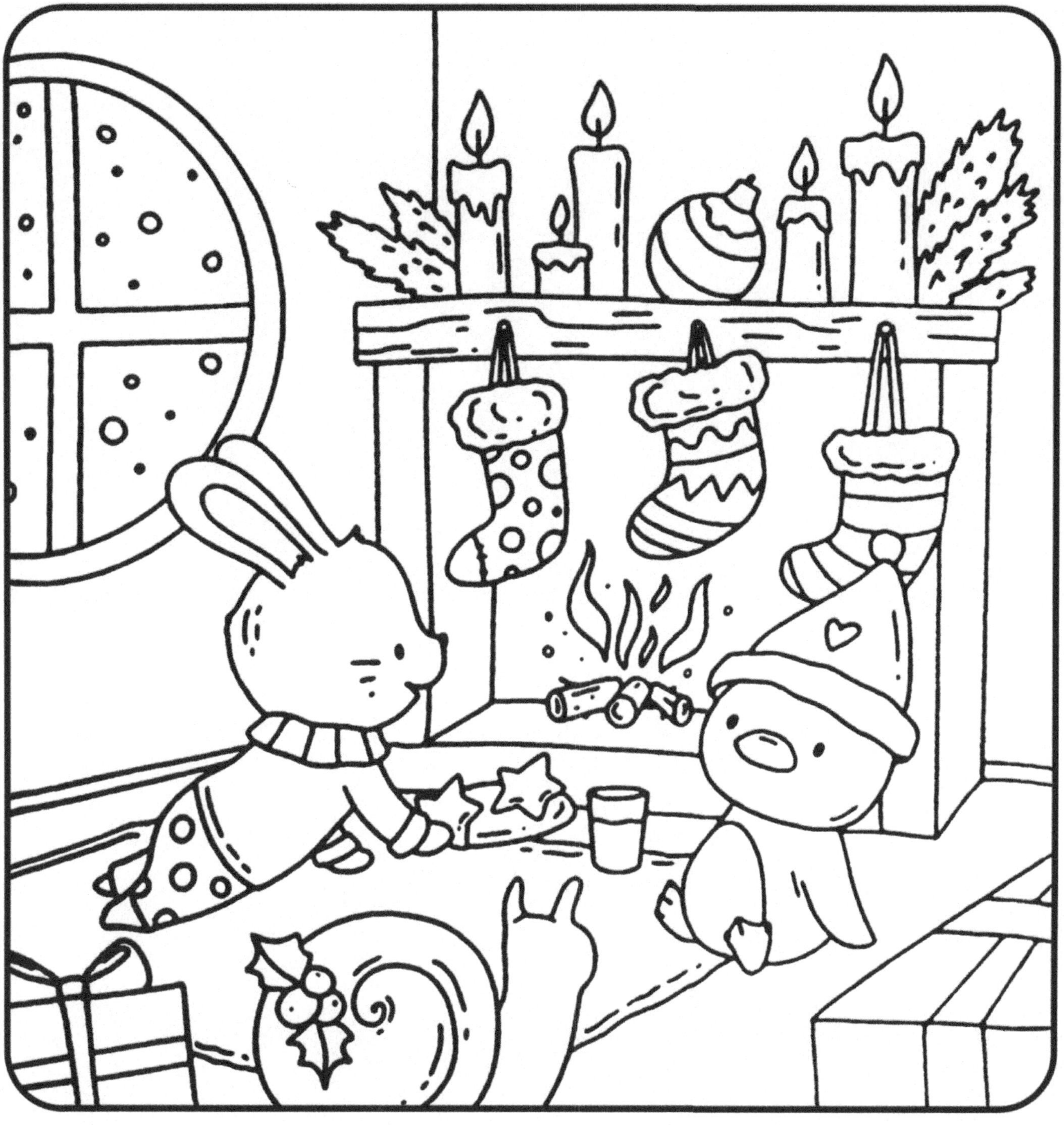

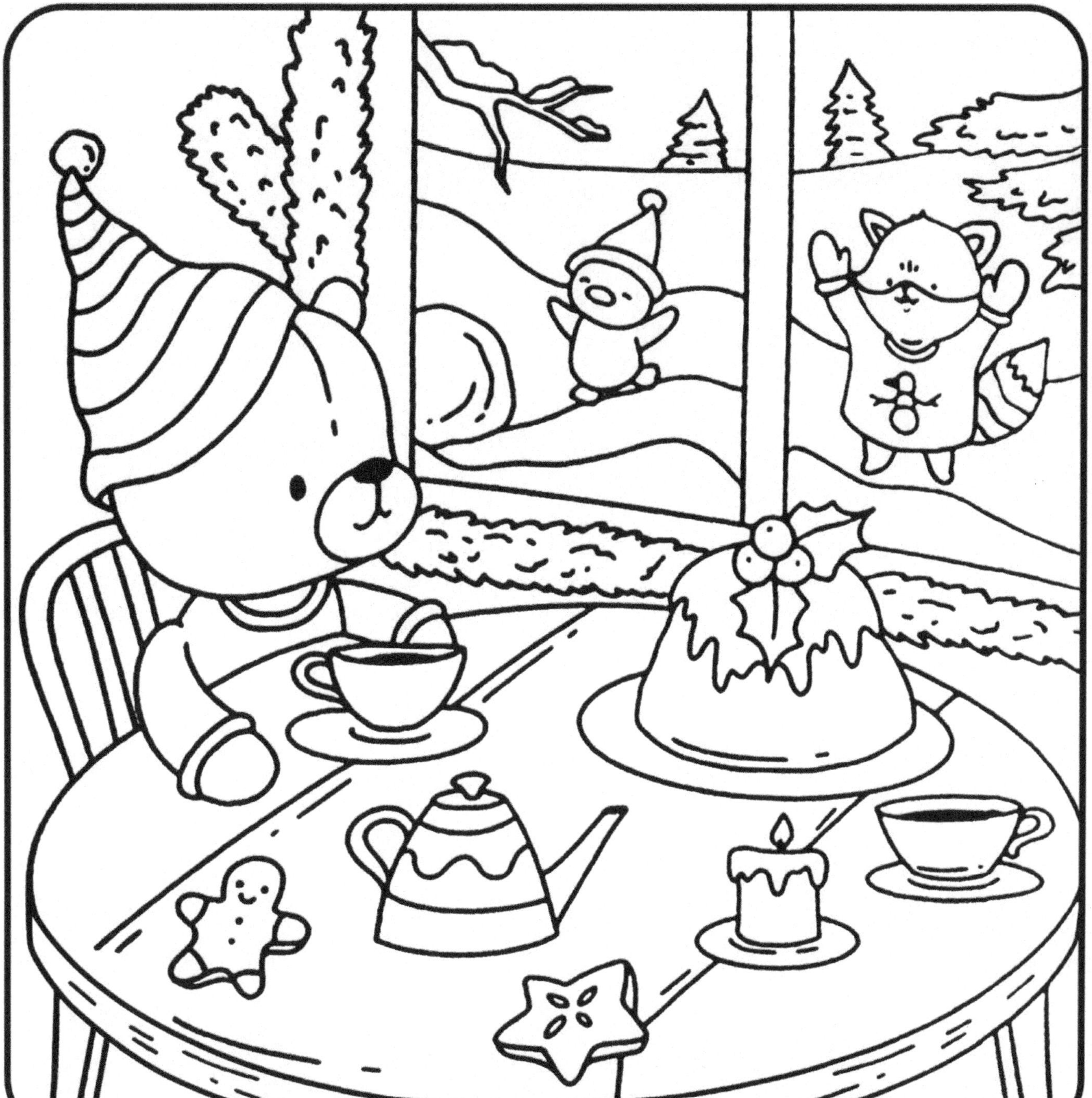

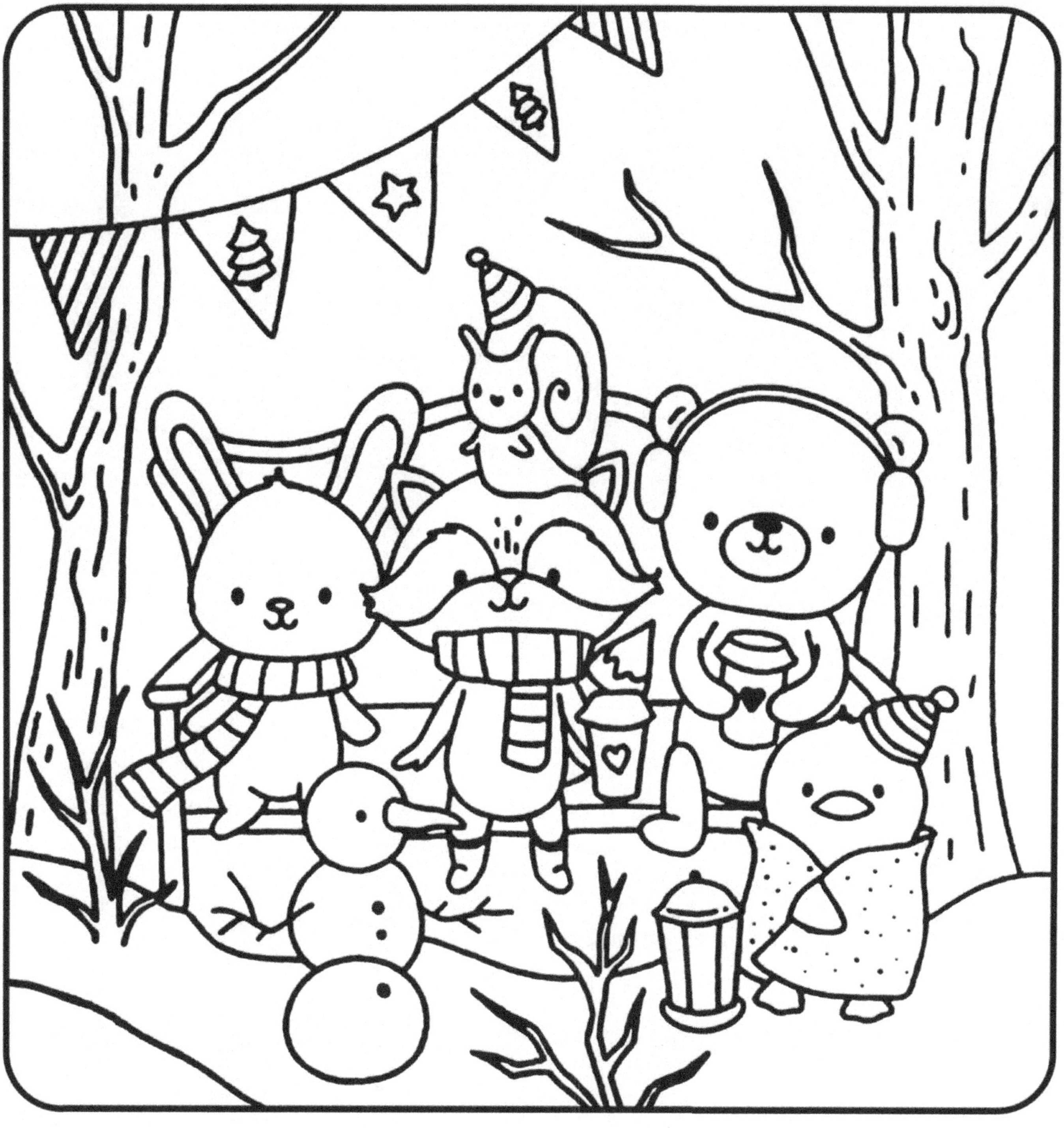

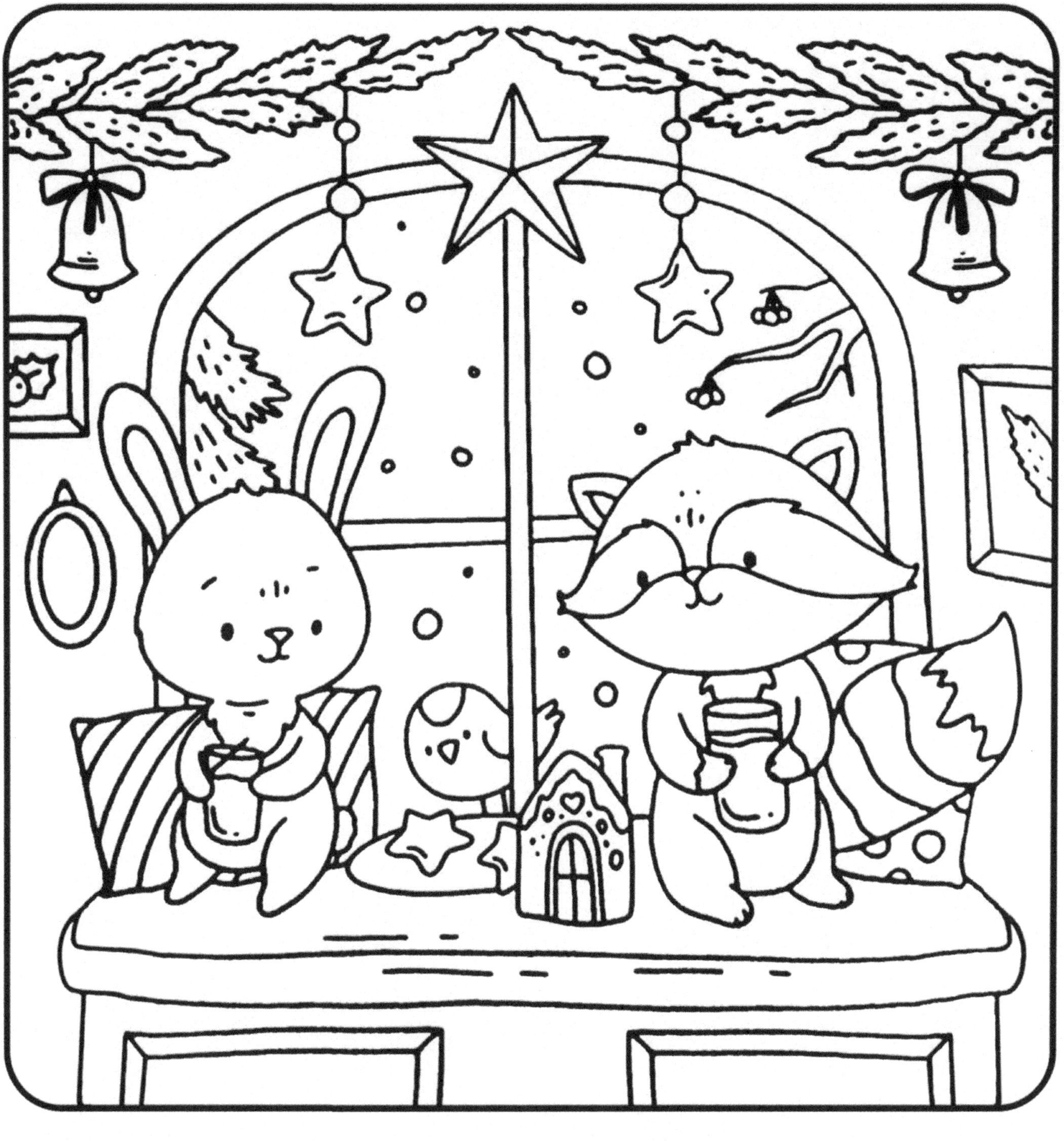

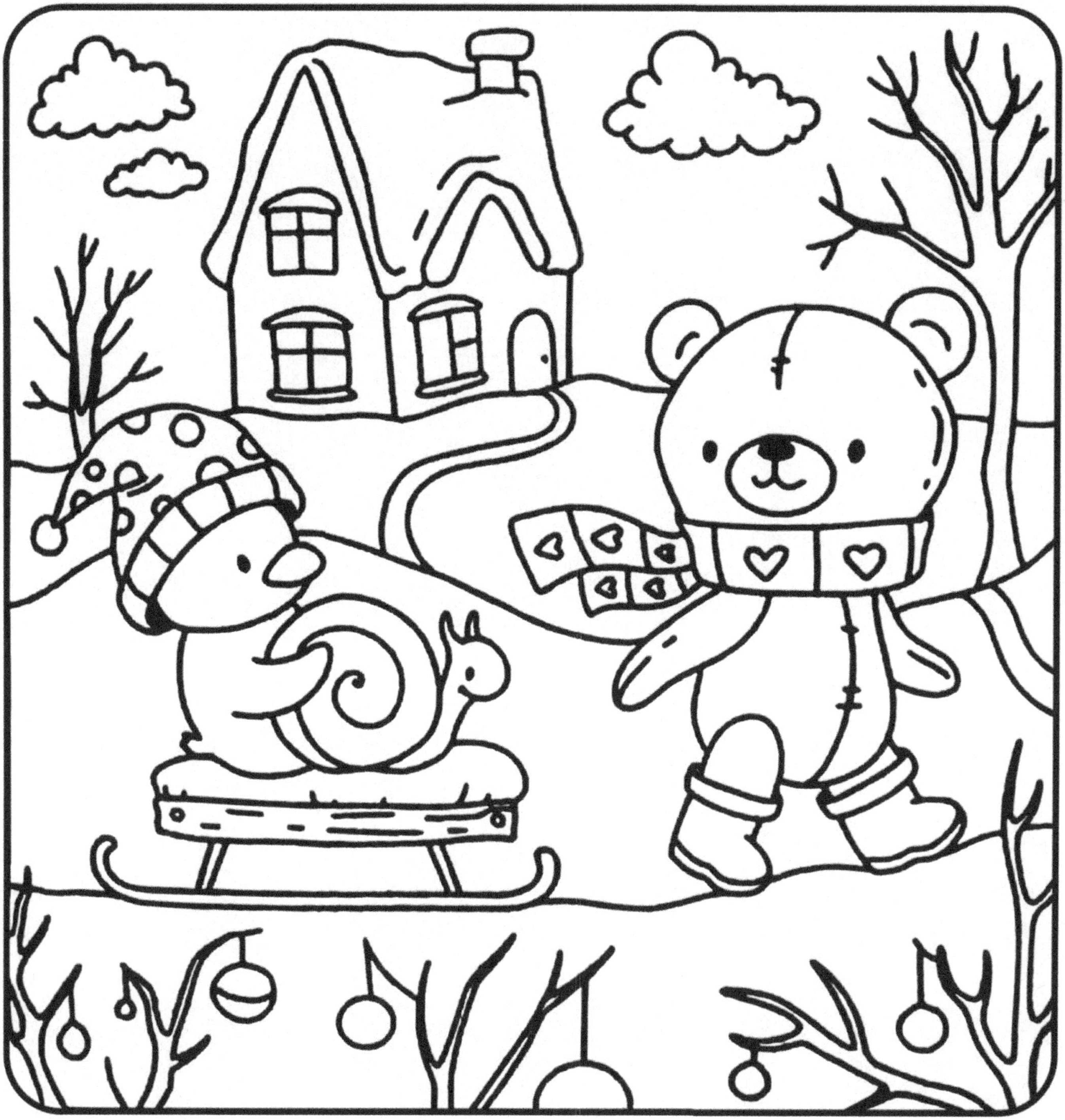

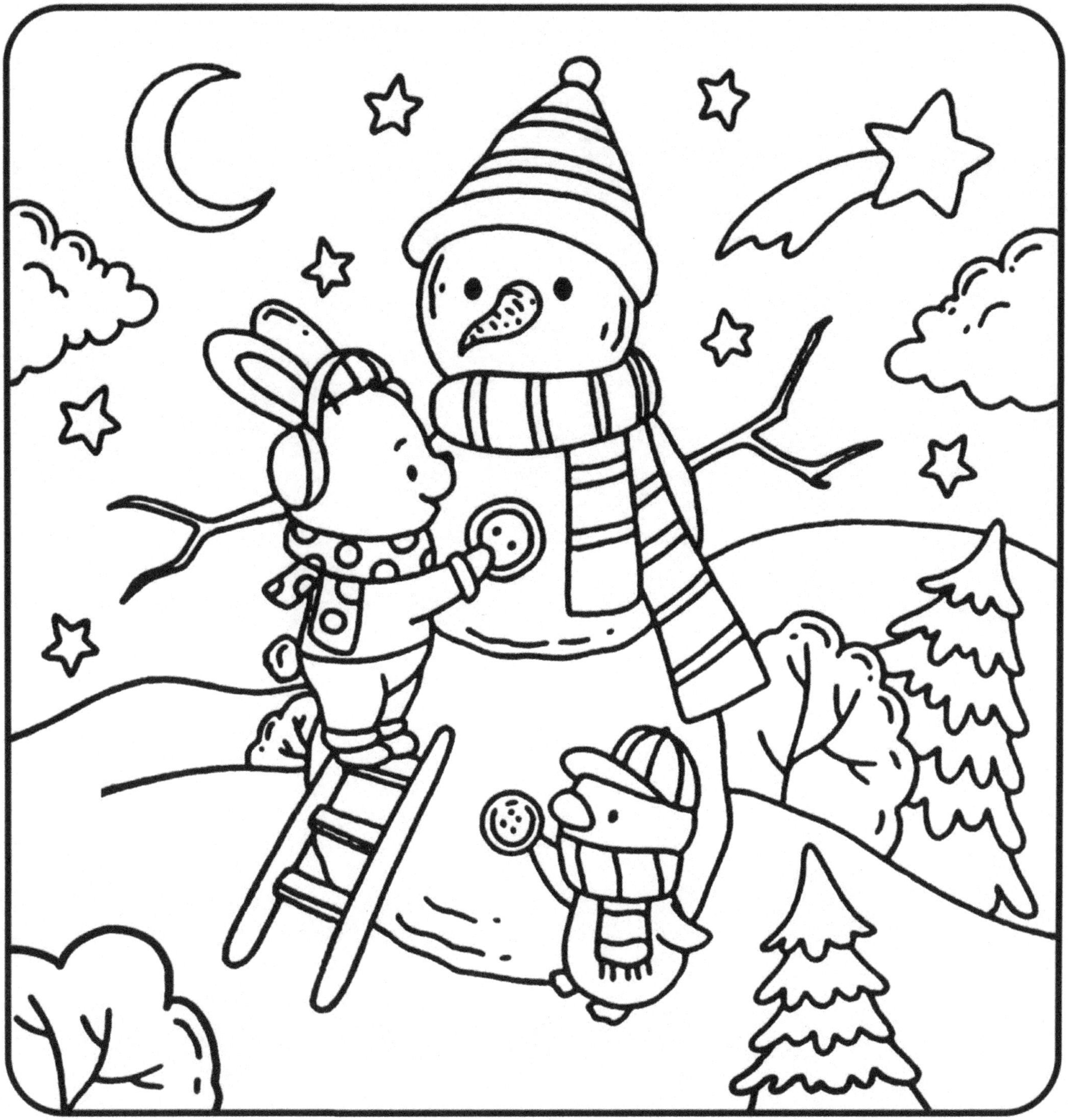

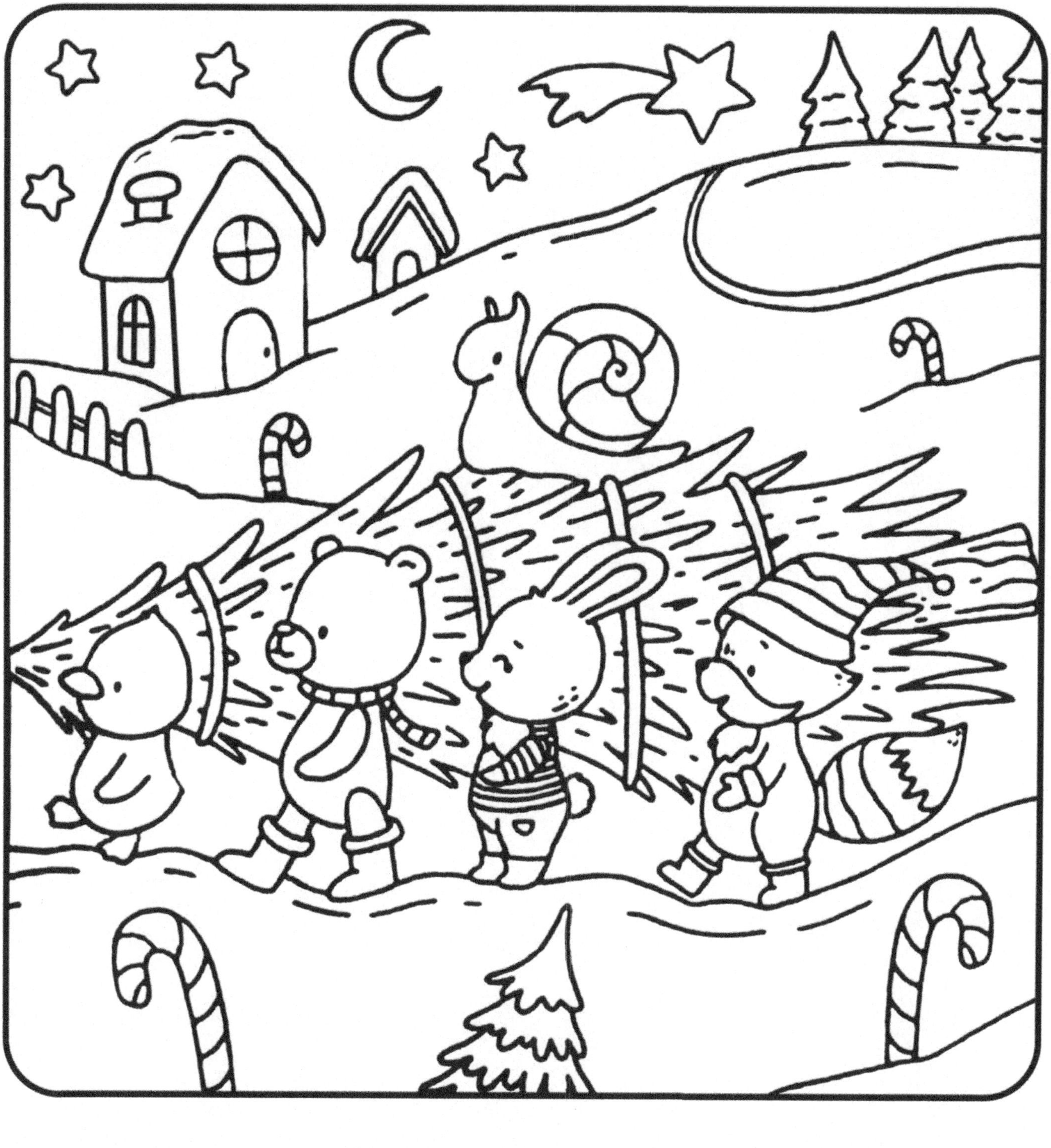

Made in United States
Orlando, FL
12 November 2024

53817267R00037